Prague
The Golden City

A book of photographs with texts about the history, art
and culture of the city on the Vltava
by Harald Salfellner

Vitalis

© Vitalis, 2003
All rights reserved
Printed in Czech Republic.
Print: Severografia, Most

ISBN 80-7253-124-7

www.vitalis-verlag.com

Contents

The author, Dr. Harald Salfellner, studied medicine in Graz (Austria) and in Prague. He is a publisher and an author and has been living in the capital of the Czech Republic since 1989. Among his publications are a number of essays, articles and books about Prague, Bohemia and Moravia that have been printed in various languages (*Franz Kafka and Prague, The Golden Lane, Mozart and Prague, Das Palais Lobkowicz, Mein böhmisches Kochbuch, etc.*).

City of a Hundred Spires

A Walk Through Hradčany

[Hradčany]

The castle and all of Hradčany (castle settlement) are situated on the left Vltava riverbank on an elongated rocky hill above the Lesser Town. "Hrad" means "castle" in the Czech language – the name of the whole area is connected with the Prague castle.

The whole castle complex belongs to the town of Hradčany also, as well as the Royal Summer Palace called Belvedere and the castle suburbs up to Strahov Abbey, which crowns the whole area.

In the castle settlements, in the immediate vicinity of the king, the most important families also lived, such as the Černíns, Lobkowiczs, Dietrichsteins, Martiniczs, Rosenbergs and Schwarzenbergs. As the building sites around the Prague castle began to disappear in the 17th century, the noblemen moved to the Lesser Town below the Prague castle.

Houses on Hradčany Square

Hradčany, viewed from the Petřín Hill

7

Hradčany dates back to 900 AD, as the first baptised Přemyslid Prince Bořivoj I transferred his residence from Levý Hradec to Prague (875). The timber built stronghold, which was at that time surrounded by a mud wall and protected with a moat ditch, received a stony church consecrated to the Virgin Mary a few years later. The son of the Prince Bořivoj I, Vratislav I, had another church built in 920 on the site of the present-day St George Basilica. Since 973, which was the year when Prague was raised to a Bishopric, during the reign of Boleslav II the castle was also a seat of the bishop.

Beginning during the times of Přemysl Otakar II, the castle was ruined and neglected and it wasn't until the reign of Charles IV of Luxembourg that the Prague castle became the centre of the Holy Roman Empire. The Gothic St Vitus Cathedral was built in Prague on the occasion of Prague being raised to an Archbishopric in 1344.

After years of desolation during the Hussite Wars in the 15th century, the Jagiello kings returned to the Prague castle with a glamorous court life after they decided to leave the Royal Court in the town centre because of street rebellions in 1483.

The Habsburgs (since 1526) enriched the castle with gardens and with the Belvedere Palace (Royal Summer Palace) and had the castle rebuilt to a more comfortable Renaissance residence.

The Castle Palaces

The large fire in 1541, when the Lesser Town and Hradčany were almost destroyed, caused huge damage. However, the building activities after the fire helped the coming Renaissance with its final breakthrough.

A new golden era for the Prague castle came with the Emperor Rudolph II of Habsburg, who made Prague a cultural and political centre of the Holy Roman Empire for the last time. The Emperor Rudolph II was an art collector and also a builder who enriched the castle and its surrounding area with magnificent Renaissance buildings.

In 1618, the second Prague defenestration was supposed to be signalled from the Prague castle and it started the Czech rebellion against the Habsburgs and also the Thirty Years War. The imperial chancellors Jaroslav of Martinicz and Wilhelm of Slawata were thrown out of the window of the Bohemian Chancellery together with their secretary Phillipus Fabricius. During the Thirty Years War, both Saxon and Swedish armies occupied the Prague castle. The valuable art treasuries of Rudolph's art collection were lost or destroyed.

The Emperor Rudolph II raised Hradčany to a Royal Town and some 150 years later, the Empress Maria Theresia declared Hradčany the fourth Prague Town.

At Pohořelec

Impressions of Hradčany

Beside the siege and damage caused by the French Army (1741) and Prussian Army (1744, 1757) in the 18th century, interesting feasts also took place in that time. For example, the canonisation of St John of Nepomuk (1729), the feasts on the occasion of the coronation of Charles VI (1711) and finally the enthronement of the Empress Maria Theresia (1743).

During the reign of her son, Joseph II, the rest of Rudolph's art collection was not enriched but even further damaged since the army used the Royal Summer Palace (Belvedere), St George Convent, Riding School and the Big Ballroom. And for the last time, an emperor used the Prague castle as his residence – it was Ferdinand V who abdicated and decided to spend the rest of his life at Prague castle, away from the Imperial Court in Vienna.

However, the Prague castle was always the seat of the supreme administration of the country and it was a representative residence of the rulers, starting with the Přemyslid Princes, later the Czech Kings, the Emperor

Charles IV and ending with the Emperor Rudolph II.

After 1918, Tomáš Garrigue Masaryk, the first president of Czechoslovakia, resided at the Prague castle. A considerable part of the reconstruction carried out in the 1920s is connected with the name of Slovenian architect Josip Plečnik. The reconstruction and research works are in operation until today. Since 1993, the president of the Czech Republic has had his seat at the Prague castle.

With exactly 203 steps, the "New Castle Steps" lead us from the Thunovská Street up the Lesser Town to the forecourt of the Prague castle. From the Lesser Town Square via Nerudova Street and via Úvoz you can reach Pohořelec and then the Strahov Abbey.

Church of the Assumption
of the Virgin Mary

Portal of the Strahov Monastery

Strahov Abbey

[Strahovský klášter, Strahovské nádvoří 1/132, Praha 1]

Strahov Abbey, Prague's second oldest religious house, was built in 1143 by the Prince Vladislav II for the Premonstratensian Order. It was originally situated outside Prague and it was brought within the town walls during the reign of Charles IV. The abbey has been frequently damaged and rebuilt during the course of history (Hussite Wars, Thirty Years War, Prussian siege etc.). Despite that, it was always one of the richest and most important abbeys in the country.

There are two churches to visit.

In the courtyard, on the left, there is the Late Gothic Chapel of St Roch, originally the Strahov parish church, built between 1603–1612 by the Emperor Rudolph II in order to express thanks for the aversion of a plaque. It is a Late Gothic building already including elements of the Renaissance style. This building is used for exhibitions today.

The second church is the Church of the Assumption with a magnificent Baroque interior. The church has the original spatial layout of a Romanesque basilica and was rebuilt in the middle of the 18th century in the Baroque style by Anselmo Lurago. Johann Anton Quittainer decorated the façade with a Baroque "Maria Immaculate"; the eyes of the statue are said to attract visitors' eyes.

Statue of St Norbert

During the Thirty Years War the relics of St Norbert of Prémontré, the founder of the Premonstratensian Order, were transferred from the protestant German town called Magdeburg, where he was an Archbishop and where he was later buried, to Prague and laid to rest in this church. Inside the church you can see the big organ which Wolfgang Amadeus Mozart played in 1787.

Between 1782 and 1784, the Old Library was supplemented by a new building containing the Philosophical Hall built by Ignaz Giovanni Palliardi. The façade of this Classical building is one of the most noteworthy architectural monuments of the Josephine period in Prague. Despite the fact that the Emperor Joseph II abolished many monasteries and convents, he approved of the reconstruction of the Strahov Abbey.

The ceiling fresco in the Philosophical Hall depicts the history of mankind and was painted in just six months by a 70 year-old artist, František Antonín Maulpertsch, in 1794.

Ranking among the most valuable decorations of the hall are the beautiful cabinets and bookshelves of walnut wood from the Moravian Monastery in Louka near Znojmo to which the whole building was adopted.

The vases and ornamentation are the work of Ignaz Platzer. There are more than 50.000 books in the Philosophical Hall;

Strahov: The Philosophical Hall of the Monastery Library with the famous ceiling painting by the Baroque Master Franz Anton Maulbertsch

The Theological Hall and Library in the Strahov Monastery

Above: The Monastery Courtyard with the statue of St Roch

however, tourists are not allowed to visit this beautiful place nowadays.

The original Early Baroque Library Hall of the monastery on the first floor, with one of the most remarkable interiors, is called the Theological Hall and was built between 1671 and 1679 by Giovanni Domenico Orsi.

The Baroque cases contain theological literature and in the glazed cabinets above the doors prohibited books ("libri prohibiti") were kept.

In the centre of the hall, there are geographical and astronomical globes from the 17th century.

Also numerous valuable illuminated manuscripts, the oldest of which is the Strahov Gospel from the 9th century, are kept at Strahov Abbey.

The abbey courtyard can be reached either through a passage at Pohořelec 8 (steps) or, by a short steep street at the western end of the square, turning left through a Baroque gateway. There are two statues of St Norbert by Johann Anton Quittainer and a nice Plaque Column.

You can also visit the Chapter Hall with beautiful ceiling paintings by A. Nosecký, where the works of the Old Masters are exhibited.

Historical folios of the Monastery Library

The bell tower, built in an Early Baroque style, contains a carillon installed by P. Neumann in 1694 which plays the Marian hymn every hour on the hour in the summer. All 27 bells were cast in Amsterdam in 1694.

Façade detail of the Loretto Church

The Bearded Virgin Mary

The Loretto Shrine
[Loreta, Loretánské náměstí 7, Hradčany, Praha 1]

According to a legend, there was a dwelling in Nazareth in which Archangel Gabriel appeared before the Virgin Mary to announce the upcoming birth of Jesus to her. The dwelling was called Casa Santa and was found in the Italian town of Loretto near Ancona and was allegedly transferred from Palestine to its present site by angels.

The Loretto shrines were founded in this country as a part of the recatholicising process after the Battle on White Mountain. Some 50 Loretto shrines were built in that time to increase the appeal of Catholicism to ordinary people.

The Casa Santa, the spiritual and architectural centre of the Loretto, is to be found in the courtyard.

The Prague Loretto was founded in 1626 by Benigna Kateřina of Lobkowicz who was a member of a rich Bohemian noble family.

After 1661 the courtyard was enclosed on all sides by ambits where the pilgrims could rest and get ready for chanting the rogations and praying.

Most visitors are eager to see the chapel in the southwestern corner of the courtyard.

One of the two Rococo altars is a famous statue of a crucified bearded woman, St Wilgefortis. This pious daughter of a Visigoth king was to be married to a pagan. To avoid the marriage, she miraculously sprouted a beard. Her father was very angry with her and so he had her nailed to a cross.

On the eastern side of the cloister is the Church of the Nativity, built by Christoph Dientzenhofer and his son Kilian Ignaz Dientzenhofer about 1735.

The interior is magnificently decorated and has a ceiling painted by Václav Vavřinec Reiner ("Presentation in the Temple"). The church represents a jewel of Baroque architecture in Prague.

The Treasury, on the upper floor of the cloister, contains vestments and valuable monstrances from the 17th and 18th centuries. There are more than 300 jewels.

The oldest piece to be seen is the Late Gothic chalice from the year 1510. The most valuable object in the collection is the famous Diamond Monstrance (Prague Sun) made in Vienna according to the design full of symbols by Johann Bernhard Fischer of Erlach in 1699. It weights 12 kg and contains 6,222 diamonds.

After the year 1918, the palace was reconstructed at great cost to become the seat of the Ministry of Foreign Affairs of young Czechoslovakia. During the Nazi occupation between 1939 and 1944, the Deputy Reich Protector had his seat here.

In March 1948, the former Minister of Foreign Affairs Jan Masaryk was found dead under the windows of the Černín palace. The circumstances of his tragic death have never been clarified and Czechs often talk about the "third Prague defenestration".

Today, the Ministry of Foreign Affairs is again seated in the Èernín palace and in the garden adjoining the palace, where you can find statues by Giovanni Santini Aichel, many concerts and theatre performances take place.

Černín Palace

[Černínský Palác, Loretánské náměstí 5, Hradčany, Praha 1]

A monumental palace (its façade is 150 metres long) founded in 1666 by Jan Humprecht Černín of Chudenice, the Emperor's ambassador in Venice, Italy.

An Italian architect, Francesco Carrati, carried out the design and the construction.

Originally, it was supposed to be a representative family palace with 30 pillars.

During the construction, there were often more than 100 people working on it at once.

After the Prussian bombing (1744, 1757) and the damage caused by the Bavarian and French armies (1742) which occupied Prague in the middle of the 18th century, the palace was restored by architect Anselmo Lurago.

The owners tried to sell the palace, even to the Emperor Joseph II, but had no success.

In 1851, the military acquired the building and it was rebuilt and converted into barracks.

As early as the Napoleonic Wars, the building housed a military hospital.

Capuchin Monastery

[Klášter kapucínů, Loretánské náměstí 6, Praha 1]

This is the first Capuchin Monastery in Bohemia, built in 1601. Adjoining the monastery is a simple Church of the Angelic Virgin Mary and inside this church there is a beautiful statue of the Holy Virgin.

At Christmas the church attracts a large number of visitors, who come to see its unique Baroque Nativity Scene.

New World

[Nový svět]

This area has characteristic picturesque small houses which were mainly inhabited by the poor and was originally a northern suburb of Hradčany, created in the 16th century.

It later became a gathering place for various artists. It has maintained its medieval character to the present day.

Over time, with the "Golden" namesake of almost all the houses in this lane, it has become a pleasant contrast to the overcrowded Golden Lane at the Prague castle.

At the Golden Grape (Nový svět 5) This building was erected in the 17th century and is guarded by a grim sculpture situated in its bay.

New World – yesterday and today

Spring and summer at the "New World"

Hradčany Square
[Hradčanské náměstí]

with the Plaque Column with a statue of Our Lady. This Plaque Column situated in the middle of the Hradčany Square was built in commemoration of the end of the plaque (1726) and the statue of Our Lady was constructed by Ferdinand M. Brokoff.

The figures of all the saints were also made in the workshop of Ferdinand Maximilian Brokoff: St John of Nepomuk, St Elisabeth, St Petrus, St Norbert, St Florian, St Charles Borromaeus, St Wenceslas, St Vitus and St Adalbert.

The Tuscany Palace (Hradčanské náměstí 5) is an Early Baroque building built by Jean B. Mathey in 1690. Since 1718, the Dukes of Tuscany owned the palace and their sculptured emblems decorate the wide front above the doors of the balconies.

The Martinicz Palace (Hradčanské náměstí 8) was built for Jaroslav Bořita of Martinicz, who was one of the two imperial chancellors who suffered the second Prague defenestration in 1618. The palace has beautiful Renaissance figural graffiti decoration depicting scenes from the Old Testament (Life of Samson) and from Greek mythology (Life of Hercules).

In the house number 10 (Hradčanské náměstí 10) lived Peter Parler, the Swabian Cathedral Master-builder.

The Marian Pillar on Hradčany Square

Hradčany Square viewed from St Vitus Cathedral

The adjoining building is the Archbishop's Palace (Hradčanské náměstí 16) This palace was originally a Renaissance building rebuilt in Late Baroque style. It has a magnificent doorway made by the French architect Jean Baptiste Mathey. There are beautiful sculptures by Ignaz Franz Platzer and five balconies. Since 1562, the Prague archbishops have resided in this palace.

The Schwarzenberg Palace (Hradčanské náměstí 2) was built between 1545 and 1563 by Count Johann Lobkowicz in a Florentine Renaissance style.

The Royal Garden
[Královská zahrada]

The Royal Garden was laid out by Emperor Ferdinand I and his successor as an ostentatious Castle Garden and now forms a part of the representative areas of the Prague castle on the site of an earlier vineyard.

Many rare plants and trees were grown in the garden and starting in 1563, tulips were grown here for the first time in Europe even before their spread to Holland. The bulbs were obtained from Emperor Rudolph of Constantinople.

Nowadays, the Royal Garden has the character of an English landscape park.

The entrance to the Royal Garden is behind the Cottage of the Royal Gardener with Renaissance graffiti.

Noteworthy are also other buildings behind the entrance, i. e. the Lion Court, built between 1581–1583 by the Emperor Rudolph II. Apart from lions, three leopards, a tiger and orangutan and other wild animals were kept there.

The Renaissance Ballroom [Míčovna], founded between 1567 and 1569 by the architect Bonifác Wohlmut was originally used for ball games. It was damaged by fire in May 1945 and restored in the 1950s.

There is also an orangery next to the Ballroom.

Idyll in the Royal Gardens

Royal Ballroom

21

The Royal Summer Palace "Belvedere"

[Královský letohrádek, Hradčany, Praha 1]

The Singing Fountain

This splendid pleasure palace was built by Ferdinand I for his wife Anna at the same time as the Royal Gardens were laid out.

The arcaded building in the style of the Italian Renaissance with its gracefully curving roof was designed by Paolo della Stela.

The upper floor was not completed until 1564.

The external colonnade is decorated with a frieze of foliage ornaments and reliefs depicting scenes from Greek mythology and a likeness of Ferdinand I presenting a flower to his wife.

Inside the Royal Summer Palace, there are two Renaissance Halls and another large room, the Great Hall, in the upper floor.

In front of the Royal Summer Palace, which is nowadays frequently used for exhibitions, there is the renowned Singing Fountain cast in 1568 (bronze) with motifs from Greek mythology.

Royal Summer House "Belvedere" in the Royal Garden

Prague Castle
[Pražský hrad]

The First Courtyard

The first and most recent courtyard, also known as the grand courtyard, can be entered from Hradčany Square through a wrought iron gateway decorated with a sculpture called Fighting Giants (1770, today a copy from 1921) by Ignaz Platzer the Elder. The first courtyard was created during the reign of Empress Maria Theresia. The gate bears the monograms of Empress Maria Theresia and her son, Emperor Joseph II.

The plans for the first, "Royal" courtyard were prepared in Vienna by the Vienna imperial Court architect N. Pacassi and Anselmo Lurago directed the work.

The gate bearing the name of the Emperor Matthias was built for him by Giovanni Maria Philippi in 1614 as a free-standing western entrance to the Prague castle. It represents the earliest piece of art in the Baroque style. In 1760, the architect N. Pacassi linked the gate with the newly built front wall of the castle. The flagpoles outside the Matthias gate are firs from the forests on the frontiers of Czechoslovakia – an idea conceived by the Slovenian architect Josip Plečnik.

To the right of the passage through the Matthias Gate, there is a staircase to the staterooms of the Maria Theresia wing, presently used by the President of the Czech Republic for official audiences. On the left, there is a magnificent contemporary staircase providing a new approach to the Spanish Hall. This grand staircase also leads to the Rothmayer Hall designed by the Slovenian architect Josip Plečnik and to Rudolph's Gallery. However, most of the other representation rooms at the Prague castle are closed for public.

A titan at the entrance to the Prague castle

The Second Courtyard

The Matthias Gate leads into the second courtyard, in the centre of which is a sandstone Early Baroque fountain, built by Francesco della Torre in 1686, with a sculpture by Hieronymus Kohl who was a famous Prague stone-mason. The wrought iron grill dates from 1702. Originally, a sculpture of the German Eagle also decorated the fountain but it was removed in 1918.

The Chapel of the Holy Rood in the southeastern corner of the Second Courtyard was built at the time of the Theresian reconstruction of the Prague castle according to a design by Anselmo Lurago. In the Chapel of the Holy Rood the famous Cathedral treasure was exhibited until 1990.

Matthias Gate

The Third Courtyard

St Vitus Cathedral

[Chrám sv. Víta, Hradčany, Praha 1]

View from the neo-Gothic central nave into the Gothic apse in St Vitus Cathedral

St Vitus Cathedral, the metropolitan church of the Archbishopric of Prague, stands on the site of a chapel that Prince (St) Wenceslas dedicated to St Vitus in 925. Later on, it became the sepulchre of the Přemyslid dynasty. In 1344, Charles IV began the construction of the present cathedral. The eastern end was designed by the French architect Matthias of Arras in an older French Gothic style. He was responsible for the choir, though only the lower part of it was completed after his death (1352). His successor, Peter Parler, enriched the structure with the upward-soaring German Gothic forms. After the Hussite Wars, during which construction was interrupted, the architect Bonifác Wohlmut topped the tower with a Renaissance steeple and balustrade, bringing it to a total height of 109 metres (358 ft).

The cathedral was to be completed in the 20th century by Kamil Hilbert and Joseph Mocker in a Neo-Gothic style.

St Vitus Cathedral is not only Prague's most imposing church and the finest building at Hradčany. It is also the city's largest church, with a total length of 124 metres (407 ft), a breadth of 60 metres (197 ft) across the transepts and a height of 33 metres (108 ft) in the nave.

Prague Castle with St Vitus Cathedral and the Royal Palace – view from the Lesser Town (Malá Strana)

Statue of St Wenceslas in St Wenceslas Chapel

During his life St Wenceslas expressed a desire to be buried in this House of God. His brother (and murderer) Boleslav had the body of St Wenceslas buried in the St Vitus rotunda. St Wenceslas Chapel was built in 1362 on the site of the saint's original grave and is the work of Peter Parler. The lower part of its walls are encrusted with over 1,300 pieces of jasper (red) and amethyst (violet) and are decorated with wall paintings (the Passion cycle) dating from 1372 to 1373. On the upper part of the walls, there are paintings depicting the legend of St Wenceslas dating from the beginning of the 16th century (the Master of Litoměřice). The tomb of St Wenceslas dates from the 14th century but it underwent some modification at the beginning of the 20th century. The Gothic statue of St Wenceslas was made in Peter Parler's workshop.

From St Wenceslas Chapel, a staircase leads up to the Crown Rooms over the south doorway in which the Bohemian Crown Jewels and insignia are kept (crown, orb and sceptre). The door to the Crown Room is to be opened by seven keys at one time only. The Crown Room is open to the public only on certain occasions, which happened only 8 times in the entire 20th century.

In the front of the high altar, there is a Renaissance Royal tomb made from white marble which is the work of Alexander Collin of 1589. In the centre of the top slab you can see the figure of Ferdinand I with his son Maximilian on his right and his wife, Anna Jagiello, on his left. On the side of the tomb are the busts of Charles IV, his four wives and his successors.

The triforium gallery runs above the arcade and below the windows of the choir. Within the triforium, and particularly, over the organ gallery, are busts of the cathedral architects, Charles IV's family and other notable personalities. These busts, mostly from Peter Parler's workshop, formed the first gallery of portraits of historical figures in Europe prior to the Renaissance. The casts of the busts can be also seen in the Royal Palace.

Medallion of Charles IV in the triforium

Neo-Gothic towers and windows with rosettes in St Vitus Cathedral

There are 21 chapels in St Vitus cathedral (St Sigismund Chapel with the relics of St Sigismund, St John of Nepomuk Chapel opposite the silver tomb of St John of Nepomuk designed by Fischer of Erlach, Pernstein Chapel (Chapel of John the Baptist) as the burial chapel of the Prague archbishops, Chapel of the Holy Cross with the entrance to the Royal Burial Vault, St Anne Chapel opposite it, with the famous wood-carving relief by Henry Bendl depicting the escape of the "Winter King" Frederick V of the Palatinate after the Battle of White Mountain, the Saxon Chapel with the tombs of the kings Přemysl Otakar I and Přemysl Otakar II, the Wallenstein Chapel situated above the vault of the famous Bohemian Wallenstein family).

Of particular importance is the Late Gothic St Wenceslas Chapel which contains the shrine of St Wenceslas and which is magnificently decorated and equipped with many art treasuries.

The Hasenburg Chapel is situated at the ground level of the tower and from there you can go up and see the bells and clocks of the tower. It is worth climbing up the 285 steps for the wonderful view you can enjoy from the top of the tower.

In the southern side of St Vitus Cathedral, there is the big cathedral steeple with four Renaissance bells. The Sigismund bell (cast in 1549) is the biggest bell in Bohemia. It is cast of bronze and weights 18 tons.

St Vitus Cathedral Belfry

The crowned "R" above the window reminds us of the legendary Emperor Rudolph II of Habsburg whose life was so closely connected to the Prague castle. Below the window, there are three stone coats of arms, the double-tailed Czech lion, the eagle of St Wenceslas (the oldest Czech coat of arms) and the coat of arms of the Prague Archbishopric.

Next to the steeple, the famous Golden Gate (Porta Aurea) is situated. On its upper part there is a mosaic dating from 1370–1371 depicting The Last Judgement. This masterpiece has undergone several restorations, the last one completed in 2000. It was carried out through cooperation with experts from the world-renowned Getty Centre in Los Angeles. There are also portraits of Charles IV and his wife Elisabeth of Pomerania on the Golden Gate.

Opposite the Golden Gate lies the Bull Staircase, designed by the Slovenian architect Josip Plečnik. It connects the third courtyard with the southern gardens, the Paradise garden [Rajská zahrada] and the garden "On the Ramparts" [Zahrada Na Valech]. Both gardens were laid out by Josip Plečnik who enlivened the gardens with different architectural works and sculptures. You can also enjoy a wonderful view of the Lesser Town, Old Town and the New Town from the gardens, which are nowadays fortunately open to the public.

St Vitus Cathedral at night

The Old Provost's House in the Third Castle Courtyard from a bird's eye-view. In front of the Provost's House is the pylon of Mrákotín granite by Josip Plečnik.

The Old Deanery

[Staré probošství]

The building of the Old Deanery, originally a Romanesque Episcopal palace, is situated at the southwestern corner of St Vitus Cathedral. It acquired its present Baroque form in the early 18th century.

The portal and the statue of St Wenceslas by Johann Georg Bendl on the corner of the building are slightly older (1662).

The Statue of St George

Near the granite monolith stands a copy of a renowned Gothic statue of St George, whose original is in the St George Convent. The statue was cast in 1373 by Jiří and Martin of Klausenberg.

The statue depicts St George on a horse, just before he slays the dragon with his lance.

The statue was damaged during a tournament in 1562 and so it is uncertain whether the current statue corresponds with the original.

The Old Royal Palace

[Starý královský palác, Jiřské náměstí 33, Praha 1]

The Old Royal Palace, the history of which is reflected in its architecture, is in the Third Courtyard. It was the Royal Residence until the end of the 16th century, when the Habsburgs transferred the royal residence and the Old Royal Palace was used as offices and storage. Part of the original palace has survived in the ground floor and basement below the present-day Vladislav Hall. The remains of the original palace were concealed below new construction under Přemysl Otakar II, Charles IV and Wenceslas IV. Vladislav Jagiello later built a new floor, in the centre of which is Vladislav Hall, the most splendid of the secular buildings in Hradčany. The entrances to the palace are on the eastern side of the Third Courtyard.

Vladislav Hall, also known as the Hall of Homage, was built by the architect Benedikt Ried between 1493 and 1503. With its considerable dimensions and its beautiful Late Gothic reticulated vaulting, it is one of the masterpieces in Hradčany. Czech Kings were elected in this hall and the President of the Republic has been sworn in here since 1934.

A short flight of steps at the eastern end of the Vladislav Hall leads to the All Saints Chapel built by Peter Parler. Notable features of the chapel interior are the cycle of paintings by Christian Dittmann depicting the life of St Prokop (1669), whose relics were transferred from the Sázava Monastery to this chapel, next Václav Vavřinec Reiner's All Saints Altar Piece (1732) and Hans of Aachen's Angels Triptych.

View into the Czech Office

Benedikt Ried built the Louis Palace that adjoins the Vladislav Hall between 1502 and 1509 for King Vladislav II. It contains the apartments occupied by the Bohemian Chancellery. From the windows of the room in the tower, the imperial chancellors Jaroslav of Martinicz and Wilhelm of Slawata together with their secretary, Fabricius, were thrown down into the castle moat on 23 May 1618. This second Prague defenestration gave the signal for the Bohemian rising against the Habsburgs and led to the Thirty Years War.

Vladislav Hall in the Old Royal Palace

The Old Royal Palace

(Former) bilingual denotation of the street

The southern doorway was made in the workshop of Benedikt Ried and is decorated with an Early Renaissance relief of St George (beginning of the 16th century).

Portal of St. George Basilica

St George Basilica

[Kostel sv. Jiří, Hradčany, Praha 1]

At the eastern end of St George Square, facing the chancel of St Vitus Cathedral, is the twin towered Romanesque basilica of St George, the oldest surviving church in Hradčany. Prince Vratislav I founded the church in 912 and its present Baroque façade dates from 1670. During renovation work in the 19th and 20th centuries, the original Romanesque character of the church was restored. The exterior is notable for its white towers and the interior for the alternation of pillars and columns and the triple-arched galleries in the thick walls over the arcades.

The raised choir has remains of Romanesque ceiling-paintings ("Heavenly Jerusalem"). The basilica became the family tomb of the Přemyslids. In front of the entrance to the crypt is a monument of Prince Boleslav II. To the right is a painted wooden tomb of Vratislav I (founder of the church).

The painted choir chapel of St Ludmila, built by Peter Parler about 1380 and containing the tomb of St Ludmila (murdered in 921, the grandmother of St Wenceslas and one of Bohemia's patron saints) is of great importance.

The chapel built onto the south wall of the church, known as the chapel of St John of Nepomuk, is also decorated with murals. This chapel was designed by F. M. Kaňka in 1718-1722. Ferdinand Maximilian Brokoff created the statue of the saint on the façade. Notable features of the interior are the frescoes and the altarpiece by Václav Vavřinec Reiner.

Adjoining the basilica is the Benedictine Convent of St George, a nunnery founded in 973 by Prince Boleslav I and his sister, Princess Mlada. The building now houses a notable collection of Gothic, Baroque and Classical Art from the National Gallery.

St George Basilica, viewed from St Vitus tower

Detail of the façade of Franz Kafka's house (Golden Lane No 22): "Franz Kafka lived here."

Golden Lane

[Zlatá ulička]

The house-sign of house No 23, "At the sign of the Guardian Angel"

Golden Lane runs between the castle walls built by Vladislav Jagiello and the Old Burgrave's House above the Stag Moat. Originally it continued on to St George Convent.

Along its north side ran the wall-walk between the Daliborka Tower and the White Tower where the famous English alchemist and charlatan Edward Kelley was once imprisoned. The north side of the street is preserved in its historic form, with tiny picturesque houses built into the arches under the wall-walk.

The Emperor Rudolph II assigned these houses to the members of his castle guard.

The lane was also called Gold-Makers' Lane and Alchemists' Lane, which refers to Rudolph's alchemists who purportedly lived and attempted to produce gold in these houses. Craftsmen and the poorer members of the community later occupied the houses.

Winter morning in Golden Lane

Kafka's little house (No 22), today a bookshop

The Golden Lane by night

In the cellar of house No 22

Probably the most famous inhabitant of this lane was the author Franz Kafka, who rented house number 22 for four months between 1916–1917 and he wrote his book "A Country Doctor" here. A small bookstore was installed here to his honour.

In house number 13, there is a staircase leading to the Daliborka Tower.

This tower was named after Dalibor of Kozojedy who was imprisoned here up to 1498. His fate inspired the famous Czech composer Bedřich Smetana to write an opera called "Dalibor". The tower was built during the reign of Vladislav Jagiello (1496) as a part of the Late Gothic castle fortification. It served as a prison almost to the end of the 18th century.

House No 19

A small garden in front of the house No 19

Loophole in the fortifications

House No 20

34

Towers within the castle fortification: Daliborka (the round tower) and the Black Tower

Eastern descent from the Prague Castle to the Lesser Quarter: The Old Castle Steps

A Walk Through the Lesser Town

[Malá Strana]

Prague gas street-lamp
from the 19th century

The Lesser Town was founded in 1257 by King Přemysl Otakar II as the second town of Prague after the Old Town. During the reign of the Emperor Charles IV, the Lesser Town grew significantly. The churches of the Přemyslid period, some of them going back to the Romanesque period, were rebuilt, and the Lesser Town was enclosed by walls which extended as far as the Hunger Wall on Petřín Hill.

The very first settlements in the Lesser Town were situated in the present-day Mostecká Street and on the Lesser Town Square.

At the time when King Přemysl Otakar II founded the Lesser Town, it was called "New Town under Prague castle", and it was later renamed to "Smaller Town of Prague".

During the Hussite Wars between 1419 and 1421, the Lesser Town suffered considerably. The Lesser Town was even burnt down by the Hussites.

A moderate revival finally began in the second half of the 15th century. Despite that, the Lesser Town was always economically weaker than the other towns of Prague.

On 2 June 1541 the Lesser Town and the Prague castle were consumed by a devastating fire that had catastrophic consequences. Over 50 people died and many charred ruins remained deserted for decades.

However, the fire led to further building. Gradually immigrants, merchants, bankers and aristocrats started to settle in this area again and built their palaces in the Renaissance style on the ashes of the ruins again. The Lesser Town prospered, especially during the reign of the Emperor Rudolph II (1576–1611). Apart from the nobility, Italian artists were particularly attracted to the area and the Lesser Town became the traditional artistic centre of Prague.

After the Battle of White Mountain and during the reign of the House of Habsburgs, whole blocks of old houses, streets and gardens disappeared to clear the way for the luxurious palaces of the Wallenstein, Liechtenstein, Michna, Nosticz, Buquoy and other noble Catholic families that built their residences in the vicinity of the Prague castle. Most of the houses and palaces were built in the Baroque style. Characteristic features of the aristocratic Lesser Town were the dome and the belfry of the Church of St Nicholas, both built by the leading architects Kilian Ignaz Dientzenhofer and Anselmo Lurago. The beauty and the charm of the Lesser Town are also characterised by numerous gardens situated on terraced slopes.

Lesser Town burghers' houses

A panorama of the Prague Castle and the Lesser Quarter with Charles Bridge

Above: Lesser Town gardens below Prague Castle (Fürstenberg Gardens)

The Lesser Town was united with the other three towns of Prague in 1784 and the Lesser Town became a district of small craftsmen, burgesses and offices. The Lesser Town fortunately remained untouched during the building activities in the 19th and 20th centuries. As a result, you can still enjoy long, quiet, romantic walks in the Lesser Town streets, which retain their original historical character as a quarter of Baroque palaces, gardens and wonderful squares.

View of the Lesser Town in winter – on the right the Church of St Nicholas, on the left that of St. Thomas. In the background is Petřín.

Lesser Town Square viewed from the St Nicholas Church

The Lesser Town Square
[Malostranské náměstí]

In the Upper Square, there is a Plaque Column with a group of statues representing the Holy Trinity according to G. B. Allliprandi's design of 1715, which was an expression of thanks for the end of the plague. Between 1859 and 1918 a statue of the Field Marshall Radetzky was erected on the Lesser Town Square and the square was called Radetzky Square at that time.

In the Lower part of the Square stands the Grömling palace (the House At the Stone Table) with a beautiful Baroque façade. In this building, the famous Café Radetzky, a coffee-house with a long tradition, existed in the 19th century. Nowadays, you can visit the Lesser Town Café on the same site.

Burghers' houses on Lesser Town Square dating from the 19th century

Former Town Hall of the Lesser Town

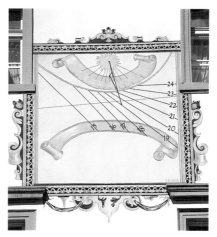
Façade detail in the Lesser Town

The Town Hall of the Lesser Town (Malostranské náměstí 21) was the administrative centre of the Lesser Town until the unification of the four towns of Prague.

Roofs of the Lesser Town houses

The Kaiserstein Palace (Malostranské náměstí 23) is a Baroque building dating from 1770. The attic contains allegories of the four seasons. The famous Czech singer Ema Destinnová lived in this house once.

Lichtenstein Palace (Malostranské náměstí 13), is a Renaissance building with a Classical façade and the Lesser Town mayors lived here until 1918.

St Nicholas Church of the Lesser Town

[Kostel sv. Mikuláše, Malostranské náměstí, Praha 1]

Western façade of St Nicholas Church

Formerly a Jesuit church, St Nicholas church occupies the site of an earlier Gothic church with the same dedication. It was constructed by three generations of the best Baroque architects of Prague. The mighty nave with its side chapels, galleries and vaulting was built by Christoph Dientzenhofer (1704–1711), the choir with its dome by Kilian Ignaz Dientzenhofer (1737–1752) and the tall tower which completed the church by Anselmo Lurago (1756).

The interior is magnificently decorated and achieves its awesome effect mainly through its superb frescos. The ceiling painting in the nave depicts scenes from the life of St Nicholas.

St Nicholas Church of the Lesser Town viewed from the Petřín Hill

Lesser Town towers, in the background the Strahov Monastery

Atlas on the Morzinský Palace

Nerudova Street

[Nerudova]

Nerudova Street is one of the most beautiful streets in Prague, named after the famous Czech poet and journalist Jan Neruda, who lived in the houses called At the Three Black Eagles and At the Two Suns. The street was once the main road to Prague castle.

The Černín-Morzin Palace (Nerudova 5) is one of the most outstanding Baroque palaces in Prague. It was designed by G. Santini-Aichel and built in 1670. Its balcony is supported by the heraldic figures of Moors and above the portal there are allegorical busts of Day and Night. The sculptures are by F. M. Brokoff.

The Thun-Hohenstein Palace (Nerudova 20) is a Baroque palace built by G. Santini-Aichel (1677–1723). Its Baroque portal is decorated with two spread-wing eagles and the figures of the Roman Gods Jupiter and Juno. The palace is connected with the Slawata Palace and the Theatin Church. The Thun-Hohenstein Palace has housed the Italian Embassy since 1921.

At Summer and Winter (Nerudova 33) – this was formerly the Bretfeld Palace, a Rococo building by J. J. Wirch dating from 1756. On the first floor there are wonderful murals. The legendary lawyer Franz Joseph Bretfeld gave dance balls here. Even Wolfgang Amadeus Mozart and his wife Constance attended a ball in this house in 1787.

Well-known house-sign in the Nerudova Street: At three fiddles

Nerudova Street

On the left and below:
The houses have mainly High Baroque façades with characteristic house emblems which served as orientation aids until 1770, when Prague houses were provided with numbers.

Commemorative plaque on the house in which the writer Jan Neruda was born

At the Two Suns (Nerudova 51)
An Early Baroque house built in 1673.
Jan Neruda, the famous Czech writer, lived here from 1845 to 1859.

Wallenstein Palace and Wallenstein Gardens

[Valdštejnský palác a zahrada, Valdštejnské náměstí 4, Praha 1]

Bronze statues in the Valdštejn Garden
(above and p. 45 above)

The Wallenstein Palace now houses the Senate of the Czech Republic. This most magnificent of Prague's noble residences and one of the first Baroque palaces in Prague was built in 1624–1630 for Albrecht of Wallenstein, one of the wealthiest noblemen of his day. He was an imperial Generalissimo during the Thirty Years War and was murdered in Cheb in 1634. Wallenstein had 23 houses, three gardens and a brickyard destroyed in order that he could build his palace facing Hradčany.

Inside the palace, the Great Hall is two storeys high and its dimensions are further enlarged artificially by means of mirror windows. The chapel, which raises the whole height of the building on the northern side, is decorated with stucco work and paintings depicting the life of St Wenceslas.

The Wallenstein gardens were laid out in an Italian Baroque style with grottoes, a pond and an aviary. Along the walks and on the fountains there are copies of bronze statues (1622–1626) by Dutch sculptor Adriaen de Vries who was working in Prague at that time. The originals were carried away by the Swedes during the Thirty Years War and are now in Stockholm. On the west side is the Sala Terrena designed by Giovanni Pieroni, with frescoes by Baccio del Bianco.

Façade of the Valdštejn Palace

44

Sala Terenna of the Wallenstein Palace

The Thun Palace (the British Embassy)

Quiet corners in the Lesser Town

View into Valdštejnská street

St. Thomas Church

St Thomas Church and St Thomas Monastery

[Kostel a klášter sv. Tomáše, Letenská ulice, Praha 1]

St Thomas Church was founded for the Order of Augustinian Hermits in 1285 and built in phases up to 1379, along with an Augustinian Monastery and St Thomas' Brewery, which began brewing the tasty Thomasbeer more than 500 years ago.

Karl Ignaz Dientzenhofer remodeled the church in the Baroque style.

In a niche over the Renaissance doorway a statue of St Augustine by Hieronymus Kohl can be seen (1684).

In the richly decorated interior are paintings and statues by Czech artists (Karel Škréta, Václav Vavřinec Reiner etc.).

Romantic idyll on the Lesser Quarter bank of the Vltava River

Vlašská Street

[Vlašská]

Hospital Under the Petřín Hill (Vlašská 36-40) is an Empire building. Standing in the courtyard is a Pieta sculpture by Jan Brokoff (1695) which was transferred from Charles Bridge to its present site in 1859. Originally, it was a hospital of the Sisters of Mercy of St Charles Borromaeus; today there is a university clinic.

Vlašská Street was named after a settlement of Italian artists and merchants who started to settle in the vicinity of the Petřín Hill during the reign of the Emperor Rudolph II.

The leader of the colony was Oldřich Avostalis, a prominent architect of the Late Renaissance. He planned the development of this part of the town, hence this area has an Italian character that can be rarely seen north of the Alps.

Also the gardens in the area of Tržiště and Jánský vršek were laid out and that is how the current Vlašská Street and Břetislavova Street originated.

Casa d'Italia (Vlašská 34) is the former Italian hospital.

In the 16th century, an Italian colony – as mentioned earlier – settled in the environs of Vlašská Street, the majority of its members being artists, who, after 1608, built this Early Baroque House with an arcaded courtyard and the Church of St Charles Borromaeus.

The church was abolished during the reign of the Emperor Joseph II and it later served as an orphanage.

Nowadays it houses the Italian Cultural Institute.

Lobkowicz Palace, viewed from the garden

The Lobkowicz Palace

[Lobkovický palác, Vlašská 19, Praha 1]

The Lobkowicz Palace, designed by Giovanni Battista Alliprandi in a High Baroque style, was altered and had an additional floor added to the side wings. The main façade is finely articulated with a massive doorway, a pediment decorated with sculpture and an attic base with statues. The interior has rich painted ornamentation. Still more interesting is the rear façade, with a cylindrical projection and a Sala Terrena leading into the grand courtyard. On the roof above the projecting bay is an unusual architectural feature – an ornamental pond.

In 1927, the Czechoslovakia gained the grand building and it later housed several ministries. It was once an Embassy of the People's Republic of China. Since 1973, the Embassy of Germany has resided in this palace.

In autumn 1989, thousands of East Germans sought help at the Embassy of Western Germany during their escape and that is how the Lobkowicz Palace in Prague entered German history. A "Trabant"(East German car) in the garden of the palace reminds us of this mass escape from the East German communist regime.

Statue on the gable of the Lobkovicz Palace

Lobkowicz Palace, viewed from the Prague castle ramp

49

Petřín Hill

[Petřín]

The southern slope of Petřín Hill (322 metres [1,057 ft]), where the legendary Czech Princess Libuše was supposed to have prophesied the glory of Prague, was covered with vineyards as early as the 12th century. The gardens originated when the "Na Nebozízku" Park and the Seminary and Kinský Gardens were united. Running between them is the so-called Hunger Wall, a part of the fortifications of the Lesser Town built during the reign of the Emperor Charles IV. On the top of Petřín Hill, there is a Labyrinth that is an intricate mirror passage, originally built for the industrial exhibition in 1891. You can also see a panorama there depicting the Battle of the Students of Prague against the Swedes on Charles Bridge in 1648. However, the biggest attraction of Petřín Hill is its Observation Tower. The tower is 60 metres (197 ft) high and was erected for the Prague Industrial Exhibition in 1891 to replicate the model of the Eiffel Tower in Paris, and now serves as a television reception tower. If you decide to climb the 299 steps, you will be rewarded with a magnificent far-ranging view of Prague and its environs.

The funicular railway to Petřín

The memorial to Karel Hynek Mácha on Petřín

Church of St Lawrence

Observation tower on the Petřín Hill

The Observatory on Petřín

51

House-sign on a house in Karmelitská
street in the Lesser Town

Wood-carving in the interior of a church

The Little Jesus of Prague

The Church of St Mary the Victorious

[Chrám Panny Marie Vítězné, Karmelitská 9, Praha 1]

The Church of St Mary the Victorious is an Early Baroque
Church, originally a Carmelite Church, which was built on the
site of an earlier protestant Hussite Church after the Battle of
White Mountain in 1620.

Inside the church, on the right-hand wall is the "Christ Child
of Prague", a wax figure (about 50 centimetres [1.6 ft] tall), originally from Spain, which the Princess Polyxena of Lobkowicz pre-
sented to the Carmelite friary in 1628 and which is still much
revered.

There are catacombs under the church.

Façade of the Church of the Virgin Mary Victorious

Access to Charles Bridge from the Kampa Island

In the streets of the Kampa Island

Kampa Island
[Ostrov Kampa]

A romantic island separated from the Lesser Town by the branch of the Vltava River called the Devil's Stream [Čertovka].

Originally there were only gardens on the island. Construction activity finally commenced here in the second half of the 15th century.

Today it is a noble and elegant part of Prague with a village-like character.

To the north of Charles Bridge, the Čertovka stream flows past a group of houses popularly called "Prague Venice".

The pottery fairs on the Kampa Island have a long tradition.

Little boats on the Kampa

Houses on the Kampa Island

Bridge Tower of the Lesser Town with former customs house

At the Stone Bridge
[U kamenného mostu]

Prague street musician

Lesser Town Bridge Towers
[Malostranské věže Karlova mostu]

The smaller tower (12th century) formed part of the defences of the Old Judith Bridge, while the Renaissance pediment and the decoration of the outer walls were added in 1591.

The other tower was built in 1464 at the behest of King George of Poděbrady. Its architecture and sculptural decoration are similar to those of the Old Town Bridge Tower.

The Gothic gate used to be closed at night.

The Club of Old Prague has its headquarters in the former customs house.

Charles Bridge at night, Hradčany and St Nicholas Church in the background

Charles Bridge

[Karlův Most]

Charles Bridge is one of the most significant structures in Prague built during the reign of Charles IV. Charles Bridge spans the Vltava River, linking the Old Town and the Lesser Town. Until the 19th century, Charles Bridge was the only connection between the Old Town and the Lesser Town.

As early as 857, there was a ferry on this site. Judith Bridge, the first stone bridge founded in 1158 replaced the former wooden bridge.

However, it collapsed during the flood in 1342. Charles IV himself laid the cornerstone of Charles Bridge on 9 June 1357. The Master builder and architect was Peter Parler who also built the Old Town Bridge Tower.

Charles Bridge achieves its powerful effect mainly through its rich sculptural decoration. On each side of the bridge, there are 15 statues. The statue of St John of Nepomuk cast in Nuremberg in 1683 and designed by J. Brokoff is of particularly great significance. Emperor Wenceslas IV had St John of Nepomuk thrown down from Charles Bridge to the Vltava River. According to the legend, St John of Nepomuk, as the main vicar of the Archbishopric, did not want to reveal the confession of the Queen Sophia.

Statue of St. Anne Mettertia on the bridge

The Cross on the Charles Bridge

Bronze statue of St John of Nepomuk

SS Norbert, Zikmund and Wenceslas

Statue of Bruncvík

Old Town Bridge Tower

[Staroměstská mostecká věž, Praha 1]

Old Town Bridge Tower, built on the first piers of Charles Bridge, forms the eastern access to Charles Bridge. It was begun in 1357 and completed in the early 15th century (the design by Peter Parler) by the Cathedral workshop.

It is considered the finest Gothic tower in Central Europe, with figural decorations which rank among the master works of Gothic sculpture in Bohemia in the 14th century. On the east side, at the top, are statues of patron saints of Bohemia, St Adalbert and St Sigismund, lower down are figures of the kings Charles IV and Wenceslas IV with St Vitus in the centre. The arch is decorated with the heraldic emblems of the territories governed by the House of Luxembourg.

The significance of the Bridge Tower is mainly in its decoration. In the Middle Ages, at a time of great illiteracy, people were more receptive to symbols and quickly understood the connections, which we must take time to decipher. The tower celebrated the Luxembourg dynasty and also hinted at the main concepts of Charles IV's political strategies. It was in fact the symbolic entrance gate to the Czech Kingdom.

Old Town Bridge Tower

View of the Vltava riverbank of the Old Town with Old Town Bridge Tower

Old Town of Prague viewed from the Lesser Town

A Walk Through the Old Town
[Staré Město]

The Old Town, the oldest of the towns of Prague, is situated in a semicircle bend of the Vltava River and therefore ideally protected. The beginnings of the Old Town date back to the first millennium. However, at that time there was no reason to call the area "Old Town". This term originated when the "New Town" of Prague was founded in the 14th century. Adjoining the Old Town in the northwestern direction, the Prague Jewish Town was developing.

The centre of the Old Town has always been the Old Town Square dominated by the Church of Our Lady of Týn and the Town Hall of the Old Town. The Old Town Square represents the centre of Prague even today. Another significant centre developed in the vicinity of the St Gallus Church [kostel sv. Havla].

During the reign of the Emperor Joseph II, the four towns of Prague – Hradčany, the Lesser Town, the New Town and the Old Town were united (in 1784) and the Prague Town Hall was located on the Old Town Square.

The Old Town underwent many changes during its rich history and some modifications happened also in the 20th century, for example, the removal of the Column of Our Lady in 1918 or the destruction of the Neo-Gothic northern wing of the Town Hall in May 1945.

Detail of façade (Art Nouveau)

North side-part of the Old Town Square

Old Town Square

[Staroměstské náměstí]

Old Town Square ranks with Hradčany as one of the most historic places in Prague and it is also one of the most breathtaking squares in Europe. The spacious square (9,000 square metres) was the market place of the Old Town in the 11th and 12th centuries and lay on the route of the traditional coronation procession of the Czech kings from Vyšehrad to Hradčany.

As the Wenceslas Square is a witness to the modern history of the country, the Old Town Square is connected with the older history, especially the burgher-houses.

The square has been the scene of great events, both glorious and tragic.

The building At the Golden Angel (Staroměstské náměstí 29) still houses the famous restaurant "At the Prince", also visited by the German writer Detlef of Liliencron during his Prague stay. The sculpture of St Florian is from the 18th century.

In the building At The Blue Goose (Staroměstské náměstí 25) there used to be a pub often visited by the German painter Carl Spitzweg.

The building At the White Horse (Staroměstské náměstí 20) once housed the Music School established by the famous Czech

Gothic arches on the eastern side

Above and below: Burghers' houses on the southern side

composer, Bedřich Smetana. In 1838 and 1839, the well-known Czech writer, Karel Havlíček Borovský, lived in this house.

At the Unicorn (Staroměstské náměstí 17): The renowned literary salon of Berta Fanta resided in this building and famous personalities, such as Franz Kafka, Max Brod or Albert Einstein, visited this place very often.

The Oppelt House (Staroměstské náměstí 3) is one of the places where Franz Kafka also lived. He wrote his famous book "The Metamorphosis" in this building.

The Štorch House (Staroměstské náměstí 16) has a beautiful façade according to the design by the Czech painter Mikoláš Aleš (Presentation of St Wenceslas). The name of the building reminds us of the builder of the house, Mr Štorch, the Prague publisher.

Above: Horse-drawn cab

At the Minute (Staroměstské náměstí 2) In this house lived the family of the Prague German-writing author Franz Kafka between July 1889 and September 1896. The three sisters of Kafka, Elli, Valli and Ottla were born here. The building has a Renaissance graffiti façade and at the time when Kafka lived there, the façade was re-painted. The sculpture of a lion on its corner reminds us of the fact that once a pharmacy "At the White Lion" had its seat in this building.

Town Hall of the Old Town

[Staroměstská radnice, Staroměstské náměstí 3, Praha 1]

The history of the Town Hall, the oldest parts of which date from the 11th century, is a story of continuing building activity, involving both the conversion of existing burghers' houses and new construction. In 1338 the King John of Luxembourg granted the citizens of the Old Town the right to build their own Town Hall. The nucleus of the Town Hall formed a house belonging to the Stein family, to which a square tower was added in 1364.

During the battles of May 1945, the Neo-Gothic northern wing and the eastern wing of the Town Hall were destroyed. Fortunately, the tower built in 1364 remained untouched. The world-known astronomical clock dating from the year 1410 was reconstructed after the Second World War.

The astronomical clock was originally installed in 1410, but in 1490, it was rebuilt by the Master Hanuš of Charles University. The clock consists of three parts – the procession of Apostles, the face that tells the time, and the calendar. The main attraction is the procession of the Apostles, which takes place every hour on the hour. Death, represented by a skeleton, pulls the rope of the funeral bell with one hand and raises his hourglass in the other. The windows open and Christ and the Twelve Apostles

Above: Archangel Michael, detail of the Astronomical Clock

The façade of the Town Hall is also decorated with a beautiful Renaissance triple-window with the inscription PRAGA CAPUT REGNI ("Prague – the head of the kingdom").

The former Town Hall of the Old Town is now used for cultural and social events, particularly wedding ceremonies, which are very popular among the Czech people.

appear. After the windows close again, a cock flaps his wings and crows and the clock strikes the hour. Other characters who also feature in the scene is a Turk shaking his head, a miser gloating over his sack of gold and a vain man contemplating on his face in a mirror.

Next to the astronomical clock, there is a decorative Late Gothic portal on the southern façade forming the main entrance to the Town Hall. The historically most valuable part of the interior of the Town Hall of the Old Town is the second floor where the most beautiful room in the whole building is preserved in its original Gothic likeness of 1470. It is the old Council Chamber with a sculpture of Christ of the beginning of the 15th century. The dominating features of the large Council Hall are two large canvases by the Czech painter Václav Brožík (John Huss before the Council of Constance and The Election of George of Poděbrady as King of Bohemia). There is also a beautiful mosaic according to the designs by the famous Czech painter Mikoláš Aleš in the entrance hall.

In the Middle Ages, there was a scaffold and a pillory in front of the Town Hall. Set into the paving in front of the east side is a stone commemorating the leaders of the Czech Protestant uprising, executed in 1621 (both Germans and Czechs, e.g. Dr. Jessenius, the Rector of the Charles University): two white swords, crossed, the date of execution and 27 small crosses.

Above: Figure of the Turk on the Astronomical Clock, symbolising paganism

The Czech Lion and the emblem on the Old Town Hall

St Nicholas Church in the Old Town

[Kostel sv. Mikuláše na Starém městě]

St Nicholas Church, originally the church of a Benedictine Monastery, now belongs to the Czechoslovakian Hussite Church. This Baroque Church with its monumental south front, long nave with side chapels and dome was built by Kilian Ignaz Dientzenhofer between 1732–1737 just on the border with the former Jewish Town. The beautiful ceiling painting depicts scenes from the life of St Nicholas and St Benedict and was painted by Peter Asam the Elder. The statue of St Nicholas on the lateral façade is by B. Šimonovský.

There is a wonderful chandelier made in Harrachov in Krkonoše.

During the reforms carried out by the Emperor Joseph II, the monastery was abolished and the church was changed into a warehouse in 1787. Later, in 1874 the church was assigned to the Russian-Orthodox Church and after the First World War, to the Czechoslovakian Hussite Church. Nowadays, concerts are given there.

Well in front of the Church of St Nicholas

73

John Huss Monument

An oversized monument was completed in 1915 on the occasion of the 500th anniversary of the death of the Czech Hussite reformer John Huss. John Huss is looking towards the Church of Our Lady of Týn where he preached and which was the Hussite bishopric church.

The Goltz-Kinsky Palace

[Kinského palác, Staroměstské náměstí 12, Praha 1]

This palace is the most beautiful Rococo building in Prague. It was built in the years 1755–1765. In 1635, the original buildings were owned by Count R. Kinsky. In the basement of the palace, there are preserved foundations of Romanesque houses. Anselmo Lurago built the palace according to the designs by Kilian Ignaz Dientzenhofer and it is considered his masterpiece. There is also a magnificent Empire staircase (1835-1836) inside the building.

Bertha von Suttner, who received the Nobel Peace Prize, was born in this palace in 1843 and spent her early childhood in the building.

Franz Kafka, the Prague German-writing author, was a student of the German Humanistic Secondary School since September 1893, which had its seat in this building. Franz Kafka was also supposed to take his final high school examination in September 1901.

Later, Kafka's father, Hermann Kafka, had his shop in the building. Today, there is a Franz Kafka Bookstore situated there.

On 21st February 1948 the Communist Prime Minister Klement Gottwald announced from the balcony of the Goltz-Kinsky Palace the resignation of the last democratic ministers and after that Czechoslovakia became a communist country.

Nowadays, the magnificent building with Rococo façade belongs to the National Gallery.

The Kinsky Palace: Detail

Kinsky Palace

The House At the Stone Bell

[Dům "U kamenného zvonu", Staroměstské náměstí 13, Praha 1]

A chapel and Gothic wall paintings were discovered recently, in the 1980s, under the 19th century Neo-Baroque façade of this house with its preserved Gothic façade from the mid-14th century. It is the only house in Prague to have been found in its original Gothic appearance. On the corner of the house there is a house-sign in the form of a bell.

Nowadays, the house At the Stone Bell is used for exhibitions and concerts.

The House At the Stone Bell

The towers of the Týn Cathedral and the houses built in front of the Cathedral

The Church of Our Lady of Týn

[Chrám Matky Boží před Týnem, Staroměstské náměstí, Praha 1]

This Gothic Church with three presbyteries was built in 1365 on the site of an earlier Romanesque Church; its façade and the high-pitched roof were built during the reign of the King George of Poděbrady (1460).

Its 80 metres (263 ft) high towers, or spires, are characteristic of the whole town of Prague.

The Church of Our Lady of Týn was then the principal church of the Utraquists of Bohemia who believed that the Communion should be administered in both kinds.

This church, in which reformation ideas were spread by the forerunners of John Huss, the preachers Konrad Waldhauser and Jan Milíč of Kroměříž as early as the 15th century and, later, also Jakoubek of Stříbro, became the principal Hussite Church of Prague.

The church belonged to the Calixtines until 1621. The parish priest and later the Hussite Archbishop Jan of Rokycany, who, along with King George of Poděbrady, fought for recognition of the Church of Czech Utraquists – the administration of the Sacrament in both ways – also preached here.

Of great cultural and historical importance is also the tomb of the Danish astronomer Tycho de Brahe who worked at the court of the Emperor Rudolph II from 1599. It is situated to the right of the high altar.

The church architecture is magnificently supplemented with the tympanum of the northern portal of the church, from the workshop of Peter Parler depicting Christ's Passion and dating from about 1390.

Especially noteworthy in the interior are the Gothic pulpit, the Gothic Madonna and the Gothic Calvary from the beginning of the 15th century.

Also a Late Gothic stone baldachin made by Matěj Rejsek, the oldest preserved Prague tin baptismal font of 1414 and the Baroque paintings are very valuable.

Of great significance on the high altar is the fine painting "Assumption" by famous Czech Baroque painter Karel Škréta (1610–1674).

The Madonna in Celetná street

A memorial desk on Franz Kafka's
native house

The Birthplace of Franz Kafka

[Rodný dům Franze Kafky, Nám. Franze Kafky, Praha 1]

Franz Kafka was born here on 3 July 1883, as the first child of six to Hermann Kafka. The house is situated on the northern side of the Old Town Square. The house is located on the edge of the former Jewish Ghetto, in the vicinity of the Baroque Church of St Nicholas. After Kilian Ignaz Dientzenhofer built the prelate's house here between 1717–1730, it served as a tenement house after the Emperor Joseph II abolished the monastery in 1787.

The building burned down in 1897 and a new house was erected on that site in 1902 and from the original house, where Franz Kafka was born, only the portal is preserved. Nowadays, the building houses a small exhibition about Franz Kafka.

In 1965, a memorial bust to Franz Kafka was placed here.

Seventy-six years after his death, the inhabitants of Prague decided to have the square in front of the house where Franz Kafka was born renamed as "Franz Kafka Square".

Building on the site of the native house on the edge of the former ghetto

At the grammar school

The Prague writer Franz Kafka

Kafka at the age of 31

Kafka with his fiancée Felice Bauer

The Powder Tower

[Prašná brána, Celetná, Praha 1]

The construction of this 65 metre (213 ft) high monument, one of the most outstanding from the Late Gothic Period and the work of the Týn School Rector Master Matěj Rejsek, was commenced in 1475 in honour of King Vladislav Jagiello.

The tower used to be called the Kutnohorská Tower, which led to the silver mining town Kutná Hora.

The Tower served as a gun powder storage site once and a wooden bridge connected the gate with the former Royal Court.

During the Prussian siege in 1757 it suffered considerable damage.

At the beginning of the 20th century, Joseph Mocker, the Cathedral Master, carried out its reconstruction.

Inside the tower, there are two richly decorated halls.

At the Golden Angel (Celetná 29):
A building from the beginning of the 19th century, once a very grand hotel, where the revolutionary Mikhail Bakunin stayed in 1848 and later also the German writer Theodor Fontane.

Celetná Street
[Celetná]

It is an important communication in the Old Town with architecturally and historically important houses, most of which were built in the Gothic period and later underwent reconstruction in Baroque style. Leading through this street in the past was the coronation procession of the Kings of Bohemia, who passed from Powder Gate to Old Town Square and then across Charles Bridge and through Nerudova Street to the Prague castle and to the St Vitus Cathedral.

Gothic Powder Tower

Mosaic at the Municipal House depicting
Princess Libuše prophesying the
glory of Prague

The Municipal House

[Obecní dům, Náměstí republiky 5, Praha 1]

This cultural and social centre of Prague, a representative Art
Noveau building, was erected on the place of the former Royal
Court in 1906–1912.

Artists such as Alfons Mucha, Ladislav Šaloun, the architects
Polívka, Balšánek and others, the whole generation of artists of
the first decade of this century tried to emphasise Czech elements when decorating the Municipal House.

Its interior houses a Smetana concert hall, a nice café in the ground
floor, a restaurant, a wine restaurant, ball-rooms and exhibition
halls.

On 28 October 1918, the Czechoslovakian Republic was proclaimed there and in 1989 the so-called round table discussion
between the former communist government and its opposition
under the leadership of Václav Havel took place there.

On Náměstí Republiky (Republic Square)

81

The Estates Theatre

[Stavovské divadlo, Ovocný trh 1, Praha 1]

This theatre was built in a magnificent Classical style between 1781–1783 in the vicinity of the Prague University.

In 1787 the world premieres of Mozart's opera Don Giovanni and in 1791 La clemenza di Tito took place there.

This theatre, originally called the Nosticz Theatre after its builder Count Franz Anton Nostitz-Rieneck, was visited by the world known Paganini, Clara Schumann, Richard Wagner and between 1813 and 1816 also by Carl Maria von Weber.

Shortly before the reconstruction of the building in 1983, the director Miloš Forman used the building for its Mozart-movie Amadeus.

Above: Statue by the Estates Theatre (the Storyteller from Mozart's opera Don Giovanni)

Theatre of Estates in the Old Town

The Bethlehem Chapel

[Betlémská kaple, Betlémské náměstí, Praha 1]

The chapel was founded in 1391 in order that sermons might be preached in the Czech language. The chapel is noteworthy for the fact that from 1402 its preacher was the Rector of the University, Master John Huss. It was from here that he spread his revolutionary ideas, which formed the ideological foundation of the Hussite Movement. Also, the German reformer Thomas Müntzer preached in the chapel in 1521.

It is no wonder that after the Thirty Years War the chapel was acquired by the Jesuits in order to remove the former heretic elements.

In 1786 the chapel was pulled down leaving only the foundations. The chapel was rebuilt in its original form and today serves as museum.

The Carolinum
[Karolinum]

The Carolinum (above) was founded by Charles IV on 7 April 1348, and it is the oldest university north of the Alps.
The original central part of the building was the Rotlöw House, donated for the purpose by Wenceslas IV.
The Gothic oriel is still preserved as part of the SS Cosmas and Damian Chapel (1370). There is a large Assembly Hall, two storeys high.

Bethlehem Chapel

The Small Square

[Malé náměstí]

This square has a quiet and intimate atmosphere. This place used to be the Prague pharmacy quarter. In its centre there is a fountain with a Renaissance grill from 1560. Since 1650, Bohemian lion has decorated the grillwork.

The oldest pharmacy in Prague had its seat in the Richter's House (Malé náměstí 11).

At the Golden Lily (Malé náměstí 12): also a former pharmacy.

At the Golden Crown (Malé náměstí 13): There is also a pharmacy in this house even today. About 1700, the famous architect and a Master Builder Christoph Dientzenhofer lived here.

At the Angel (Malé náměstí 1): Angelus of Florenz, the court pharmacist of the Emperor Charles IV worked here.

At the White Lion (Malé náměstí 2): Take note of the Gothic portal with a lion symbol and the rococo-relief depicting the Christ's resurrection.

U Rottů (Malé náměstí 3): Its façade is decorated with ornaments and figural scenes painted according to cartoons by famous Czech artist Mikoláš Aleš. In 1488, the first Czech Bible was printed in this house.

Czech lion on a fountain
at the Small Square

Little Square, the former Apothecaries' Quarter

Mariánské náměstí

[Mariánské náměstí]

The southern side of the square is enclosed by a garden wall of Clam-Gallas Palace where you can find a sculpture called Vltava, based on the Vltava River, made by Václav Práchner in 1812. This sculpture is popularly called Terezka.

The Municipal Library (Mariánské náměstí 1) is a modern building built by František Roith in the 1920s.

The official representative residence of the mayor of Prague who is called "primátor" in Prague is there.

Also a puppet theatre is seated in the house.

The New Town Hall (Mariánské náměstí 2) is a Late Art Noveau building from 1912 decorated with sculptures by Ladislav Šaloun and Josef Mařatka.

The building is the seat of the Mayor of Prague.

On the corners of the New Town Hall you can admire two sculptures by Ladislav Šaloun: The Black Rider and Rabbi Loew ben Bezalel.

Girl at the Well – Terezka

The New Town Hall on Mariánské náměstí

The Clam-Gallas Palace

[Clam-Gallasův palác, Husova, Praha 1]

This most outstanding Baroque palace was built by the Viennese Court Architect Johann Bernhard Fischer of Erlach for the wealthy patron of the arts, Jan Václav Gallas between 1713–1719.

A wonderful harmony of architecture and plastics was created there. There are two massive statues of giants of its two portals made by the Master Matthias Bernhard Braun.

In the first courtyard you can find a statue of Triton on the fountain.

In one of the most precious staircase-houses in Prague that leads to the 3rd floor and there are the frescos by Carlo Carlone. Filip of Clam once owned the palace, hence its name Clam-Gallas Palace.

The Clam-Gallas Palace today houses the Municipal Archives of Prague, and its rooms contain documents, municipal books, historical materials, photographs, graphic sheets, maps and signets.

Above: The façade of the Palace

Atlases on the portal

Small sandstone angels above the stairs

86

Rotunda of the Holy Cross

[Rotunda sv. kříže, Anenské náměstí, Praha 1]

This rotunda was built as a graveyard chapel in the 12th century. It is only because of the efforts of a group of artists in the 19th century that this Romanesque jewel was not levelled to the ground. At that time, the rotunda was restored and the Gothic wall paintings from the 14th century fully exposed. The design of the iron-fountain outside the rotunda is by famous Czech painter Josef Mánes.

The Smetana Museum

[Smetanovo muzeum, Novotného lávka, Praha 1]

This building housed the Prague waterworks once. Its façade was decorated in the style of the Czech Renaissance after the design by Antonín Wiehl of 1885. In 1936 the Smetana Museum was established in the building, since the famous Czech composer Bedřich Smetana lived here between 1861–1863 and composed his famous opera The Bartered Bride [Prodaná nevěsta] here. There is also a Bedřich Smetana memorial erected in 1984 in front of the museum.

Rotunda of the Holy Cross

Novotného lávka on the Old Town Vltava riverbank

The Czech Lion on the Bridge Tower

Křížovnické náměstí

[Křížovnické náměstí]

The charming square originated on the bridgehead of the Charles Bridge in the 16th century.

It is bounded on three sides by the church of St Francis, the church of St Salvator and the Old Town Bridge tower which is believed to be one of the most beautiful bridge towers in Europe.

You can enjoy a charming view of the Prague castle, the Vltava River and the Lesser Town Bridge Tower.

Křížovnické Square
with the St. Salvator Church

The Eagle in the emblem

The Monastery and Church of the Knights of the Cross with Red Star

Statue of Charles IV

Above: View from the Mánes Bridge

The monument to the Emperor Charles IV with allegories of the four university faculties and the figures of the famous contemporaries (i.e. the cathedral Master builder Matthias of Arras) was erected in 1849 to commemorate the quincentenary of the founding of the Charles University. The statue was cast in Nuremberg, Germany.

"Theologia" (detail)

The Church of the Knights of the Cross with a Red Star and of St Francis Seraphicus

[Kostel sv. Františka Serafínského, Křížovnické náměstí, Praha 1]

This Baroque building with a magnificent dome was built in 1679–1689 after plans by the Burgundian architect Jean B. Mathey. The Order of the Knights of the Cross with a Red Star originated as the only Czech ecclesiastical Catholic order. The church should resemble St Peter Church of Rome.

On the façade of the church there are statues of angels and Czech patron saints and in front of its entrance the statues of the Virgin Mary and St John of Nepomuk.

Inside the church, you can find painting by Václav Vavřinec Reiner – the Last Judgement.

Standing by the corner of the Church of St Francis is a Baroque viniculture column with a statue of St Wenceslas by the sculptor J. J. Bendl dating from the year 1676 which was transferred to its present site from the centre of the square in 1847.

The members of the order, who lived since 1252 according to the rules of St Augustinus, were responsible for the maintenance of the former Judith Bridge and for the taxes as well. This right of theirs ensured them their only income source. They were famous for their church music; even Antonín Dvořák played the organs here. One member of the order, who came from the vicinity of Znojmo and was called Karl Postl, became later on a famous author, Charles Sealsfield being his pseudonym.

St Salvator Church

St Salvator Church

[Kostel sv. Salvátora, Karlova, Praha 1]

St Salvator Church was originally a Jesuit church within the Clementinum complex. It was rebuilt in Renaissance style at the end of the 16th century. The Baroque porch was added in the 17th century.

The statues of the saints are made by Johann Georg Bendl. The towers were built 1714. In the church crypt, Bohuslav Balbín, the Jesuits historian, is buried.

The bell-tower of the Clementinum

The Clementinum

[Klementinum]

Formerly a Jesuit college was built between 1653–1723 on site of 32 houses, 3 churches, 7 courts and several gardens. After Prague castle, it is the largest complex of buildings in Prague.

The Church of St Clemens built by Kilian Ignaz Dientzenhofer belongs to the Clementinum complex, as well as the Church of St Salvator.

The Emperor Ferdinand I had the Jesuits called to Prague in 1556. After their arrival to Prague, the Jesuits established their main seat in the former Dominican monastery at St Clement together with schools, libraries, a theatre and a printing house.

The Clementinum was supposed to be the Catholic counter pole to the Protestant-oriented Charles University.

A Prague student in the Clementinum

The western façade of the Clementinum

After the Battle on the White Mountain in 1620, the Jesuits attached Charles University to their college, renaming it as the Charles-Ferdinand University.

However, during the reign of Joseph II, even the Jesuits had to leave Prague and the Clementinum complex became the Archbishop seminar.

Nowadays the Clementinum is the seat of the National and University Library and in the beautiful Mirror Chapel very often concerts are held. In the first courtyard there is a sculpture of a Prague student to commemorate the students who helped to defend Prague against the Swedes in 1648.

Karlova street, formerly Jezuitská street

At the Golden Well (Karlova 3)
A Renaissance house with
a façade wonderfully decorated
in Baroque style.

A Walk Through the Jewish Town

[Pražské židovské město]

No one dares to say when exactly the Jews came to Bohemia; the beginnings are still in the darkness.

Since the Middle Ages lived Jewish merchants, doctors and officials in Prague.

In the 10th and 11th centuries, there were two main Jewish settlement areas, the first one below the Prague castle area (Hradčany) and the other at Vyšehrad.

After 1100, the Jews lived in the surroundings of the Spanish Synagogue (Altschul [Old School]).

The famous Prague Jewish Ghetto developed at the end of the 12th century.

A golden era for the ghetto was during the reign of Rudolph II, whose Minister of Finance was the mayor of the Jewish Town called Mordechai Maisl. He had the streets of the ghetto paved, the Jewish Town Hall and Maisl Synagogue built and the Old Jewish Cemetery called "Bethchajim" (The house of life) established which now attracts so many visitors.

About the same time, another notable inhabitant of the ghetto was the High Rabbi Loew, a theologian and a student of Cabbala who features in many legends and is said to have created the Golem (an artificial human being). Golem helped the Jews when they suffered.

At Easter 1389, the Prague Jewish Ghetto was ravaged by one of the most terrible pogroms in the whole history of the ghetto. The walls of the Old-New Synagogue were soaked with the blood of the murdered Jews.

The Jewish inhabitants were driven away from Prague two times. In 1541 during the reign of Ferdinand I and then under the Empress Maria Theresia in 1744. She forced them by means of a decree out of Bohemia. Three years since the time when the Jews left Prague, the Empress was forced to take her decree back.

Her son Joseph II made the old Jewish Town the fifth ward of the towns of Prague. Thereafter it became known as Joseph's Town.

The greatest threat the town experienced was at the end of the 19th and the beginning of the 20th centuries. The magistrate intended to pull down the old buildings during the clearance activities. According to the original plan, there was supposed to be a wide avenue from the Wenceslas Square through the Old Town Square down to the Vltava River.

The only part of this project that was carried out was the construction of Pařížská Street, laid out on the site of the almost completely demolished Prague Jewish Town.

The Prague Jews had a final deathblow waiting for them – nearly 80,000 Jews from the "Protectorate Bohemia and Moravia" lost their lives during the occupation years 1939–1945, most of them under tragic circumstances.

The Jewish Museum founded in 1906 houses a unique collection of different objects and documents, which are exhibited in several buildings and synagogues. On Saturdays, however, is the Jewish Museum and the synagogues as well, closed due to Sabbath holiday.

The Old-New Synagogue

[Staronová synagoga, Červená, Praha 1]

The Old-New Synagogue is today the oldest synagogue in Europe, which is still in use for worship. It was built about 1270 in Early Gothic Style and ranks among the oldest preserved Gothic monuments in Prague in general. The origin of the name Old-New is unclear and is interpreted in many ways. The oldest part is the Early Gothic south hall, originally the main hall of the synagogue to which a two aisled hall in Cistercian Gothic style was added in the 13th century. Against the southern wall, there is the entrance portal with a tympanum from the 14th century decorated with a grapevine symbolising the 12 Israelite tribes. Also dating from the 15th century are the two brick-built gables. The galleries for women were completed in the 17th and 18th centuries only.

Above: The legendary Golem, closely linked to the Old-New Synagogue

The interior of the synagogue is richly decorated and the double nave is roofed with what in this country is a unique quintpartite vault (with five ribs in each bay). Situated on the eastern wall is an altar with a shrine (Aron-Hakodesch) for the Torah (parchment rolls of the Five Books of Moses). The pulpit (almemar), separated from the rest of interior by a wrought-iron grill of the 15th century dominates the centre of the synagogue. Also of interest is the historical banner of the Prague Jewish community. At the beginning of the 14th century a vestibule was built to the original building of the synagogue in which two treasure chests were placed in the 17th century for the tax collectors.

The Jewish Town Hall

[Židovská radnice, Maiselova 18, Praha 1]

The Jewish Town Hall was built in the eighties of the 16th century by the architect Pankras Roder and financed by Moradecai Maisl. Its present Rococo appearance is the result of a reconstruction carried out in 1763. It is situated in the vicinity of the Old-New Synagogue. Also dating from that time is the wooden tower and clock with a Hebrew figures, the hands go anti-clockwise since Hebrew is read from right to left. The Jews do not have numbers, numerical values are indicated by letters of the Hebrew alphabet in the manner of Old Latin.

The Jewish Town Hall houses the Council of Jewish Religious Communities, the administrative centre of the Prague Jewish Community and a ritual dining room. You can also see there an exhibition of wonderful ritual textiles (curtains from synagogues of Europe). After the Swedish siege in 1648 were the Jews as a reward for the achieved deeds during the siege allowed to build a tower at the Town Hall.

In the neighbourhood of the Jewish Town Hall, there is the Town Hall Synagogue, often called, the High Synagogue, where you will find the prayer area, which is in a beautiful Late Renaissance Hall in the second floor.

The Maisl Synagogue

[Maiselova synagoga, Maiselova 10, Praha 1]

This synagogue was founded in 1590 by Mordechai Maisl, the mayor of the Jewish Town in the time of Rudolph II, as a family place of prayer.

It is a three-aisled Renaissance building with 20 columns supporting the roof. There was a large devastating fire in 1698 and then it was remodelled in Neo-Gothic style at the end of the 19th century.

During the Nazi-occupation, the synagogue served as a warehouse for the confiscated furniture and objects from the houses of the deported Jews.

Nowadays, the synagogue houses an interesting exhibition of silverware objects used in the synagogues. Especially of great interests are the different "pointers" made from ivory, wood, metal etc., which were used for reading the Torah.

Ceremonial Hall in the Jewish Town

The Ceremonial Hall

[Obřadní síň, U Starého hřbitova 3a, Praha 1]

To the right of the entrance to the Old New Cemetery is the Neo-Romanesque Ceremonial Hall (1906) which is used for special exhibitions.

On permanent display here are children's drawings from the Terezín concentration camp. Most of the child-artists were deported to the Auschwitz termination camp in 1944 and only few of 15,000 children survived.

The Pinkas Synagogue

[Pinkasova synagoga, Široká, Praha 1]

The original building from the 11th century was said to be the oldest synagogue in Prague.

On the site of the synagogue, which belonged to the Rabbi Pinkas in the 14th century, a place of worship was founded in 1535. In 1625, it was reconstructed in a Late Renaissance style.

In the 1950s, the synagogue became a memorial place to all 77,297 Jewish victims of the Nazi persecution. Their names are inscribed alphabetically on all the walls of the synagogue as an eloquent witness of that time. The names were collected from the transport documents.

The Pinkas Synagogue

The Old Jewish Cemetery

[Starý židovský hřbitov, Široká, Praha 1]

The Old Jewish Cemetery in Prague is today the second oldest (after the cemetery in Worms, Germany) undamaged Jewish cemetery to survive the period of the Nazi occupation. The first references about it date back to the first half of the 15th century. The cemetery remained in use until 1787. Under its elder trees there are no fewer than 20,000 gravestones. The restricted area of the cemetery inadequate for the large number of burials, and additional earth had to be brought in for more graves. The result is that in places there are up to twelve superimposed layers of burials. Hence the extraordinary accumulation of gravestones, huddled together in picturesque confusion.

Below: the Spanish Synagogue [Španělská synagoga, Vězeňská 1]

The oldest gravestone is that of the scholar and poet Avigdor Kara (died in 1439) who lived through the pogrom of 1389 and wrote an elegy on it. A Renaissance sarcophagus carved with the figures of lion marks the tomb of the learned Rabbi Jehuda Loew ben Bezalel (died in 1609). Other notable graves are those of Mordechai Maisl who was the mayor of the Jewish Town (died in 1601), the historian and astronomer David Gans (died in 1613) and the learned Joseph del Medigo (died in 1655). One of the most beautiful and richly decorated is that of Heudele Basse-vi (died in 1628), the wife of Jakob Bassevis, Treasurer of the Wallenstein family. The last funeral took place in 1787 since the Emperor Joseph II prohibited further funerals due to hygienic reasons. The pebbles accumulated on many of the graves together with pieces of paper expressing different wishes are deposited by the visitors of the cemetery.

The synagogue was built after the year 1882 and reminds us of the Jews who had fled from Spain and settled in Prague. It was given its present Moorish-style imitating the Spanish Alhambra with rich gilt stucco decoration. This synagogue used to be the centre of the Jews of the eastern rite. Today it houses a collection of ritual Jewish textiles. In 1836 became the synagogue a Reformed one and an organ was installed in the interior. The first organist was František Škroup who composed the Czech national anthem "Kde domov můj" ("Where is my homeland").

The House of Artists

[Dům umělců, Náměstí Jana Palacha, Praha 1]

It is one of the most outstanding Neo-Renaissance buildings in Prague. It was originally called the Rudolfinum after the Crown Prince Rudolph.

The "Prague Spring" concerts take place there. Between 1918–1939 the Czechoslovakian Parliament was placed in this building.

There are also statues of notable composers, such as Wolfgang Amadeus Mozart and Felix Mendelssohn-Bartholdy. There is also a memorial to the Czech painter Josef Mánes.

The Lesser Town is to be reached through the elegant Mánes Bridge from here.

In front of the building there is a statue of the famous composer Antonín Dvořák.

A Walk Through the New Town

[Nové město]

The New Town of Prague was founded in 1348 by Charles IV who incorporated in its area a number of older communities. It is actually a young part of Prague in comparison with the Old Town or with Hradčany and their 1000 years history. Charles IV wanted to acquire a new territory for the constantly developing town and to use this opportunity to move out of the Old Town some of the crafts and trades which disturbed its original surrounding.

However, we must not forget that as we pass the facades of the 19th and 20th century houses we walk along the same streets that were laid out on the orders of the Emperor Charles IV. He also prescribed the position of the churches, which had to be built from stone.

Nowadays, the New Town as a whole is not particularly attractive to tourists because it has always tried to be modern. The New Town has even today this very young atmosphere characterised by the life of a modern city. Many significant companies have their offices there and many political and cultural revolutions took place there, especially in the 20th century.

The expensive and noble New Town with the Wenceslas Square as its centre is characterised by elegance and style does not remind us at all of the fact the New Town was the centre of the revolutionary Hussite Movement once.

The Hussites started their uprising just in the New Town.

"Upper New Town" was called the residential area Vinohrady where you can feel the elegance of the past periods.

There are also noteworthy buildings to be visited: St Ludmila Church built between 1888–1893 by Joseph Mocker and the Church of the Holy Heart on the Jiřího z Poděbrad Square built by Josip Plečnik between 1928–1932.

Hotel Zlatá Husa (Václavské náměstí 7): Prague hotel with a long tradition.

On the right: Crown [Koruna] Palace (Václavské náměstí 1)
This Art Noveau building housed a big, at that time very modern cafeteria (buffet) after the First World War. A meal could be purchased there for a very reasonable price of 1 Czechoslovakian Crown. On the top of the building erected in 1912, there is a crown, which gave the name to the palace. The building, which stood on this site earlier, housed a coffee-house "Edison" allegedly also visited by the famous inventor during his stay in Prague.

Below: Charles Square

Wenceslas Square

[Václavské náměstí]

It is the main and largest boulevard, a shopping centre and a centre of modern Prague, surrounded by cinemas, office blocks, renowned hotels, restaurants and cafés. This square was called the Horse Market until 1848, when Karel Havlíček Borovský, famous Czech writer and journalist, suggested its recent name. The square is 750 metres (2,462 ft) long and 60 metres (197 ft) wide.

The square played an important role in the history of Prague – 1945, 1968 and especially on 28th October 1918, when the Czechoslovakian Republic was proclaimed there. The German writer Detlef of Liliencron called the Wenceslas Square "the proudest boulevard of the world".

The Lucerna Palace (Václavské náměstí 38) was built by the father of the President Havel. It is an Art Noveau building of 1912 with a passage leading to Vodičkova Street and Štěpánská Street. During World War I it used to be the centre of Prague social life and balls took place there very often.

In the insurance palace Assicurazioni Generali (Václavské náměstí 19) Franz Kafka started his career as an insurance employee.

The Grandhotel Europe
(Václavské náměstí 27)
This Art Noveau building built in 1906 houses a beautiful café where Franz Kafka read from his book called "The Metamorphosis".

The National Museum

[Národní muzeum,
Václavské náměstí 68, Praha 1]

The imposing building stands at the upper part of the Wenceslas square and its main front is more than 100 metres (328 ft) long. It was built between 1885–1890 by Joseph Schulz in a Neo-Renaissance style and is more than 70 metres (230 ft) high. Until 1875 the so-called Horse Gate occupied this site. This building is of great symbolic meaning to the Czech people.

Its hall, façade, staircase and ramp are decorated with sculptures made by famous sculptors. On the ramp of the National Museum, there is a statue of Bohemia and next to it stands a young girl (it symbolises the Vltava river) and an old man (the Elbe [Labe] river). There are also statues of Moravia, Silesia and naturally Bohemia as a benefactress of arts and science. At the main dome, there are allegorical statues made by Bohuslav Schnirch symbolising the Devotedness, Enthusiasm and Love of the truth and of the past.

One of the most valuable departments of the museum is a library containing almost one million volumes and outstanding medieval manuscripts. On the 1st floor, you will find history exhibitions and in the 2nd floor you can visit the scientific, mineral and geological departments. Especially noteworthy are the mineral-geological collections of the French geologist Joachim Barrande.

St Wenceslas Monument

In the middle of the Wenceslas Square once stood a statue of the Prince Wenceslas made by J. G. Bendl, which was in 1879 transferred to Vyšehrad. The current monument is the work of Josef Václav Myslbek erected in 1912–1913. The statue represents St Wenceslas on a horse and at the foot of the pedestal, there are sculptures of Czech patron saints – St Ludmila, St Procopius, St Agnes and St Adalbert. Lot of historical events is connected with this statue and so it became the most favourite meeting point in Prague.

Prague Opera House
(former New German Theatre)

[Státní opera, Wilsonova 4, Praha 1]

Already in 1859, there was a wooden building on this site, which was used only during the summer time as a New Town Theatre. The today's Neo-Rococo building was built around 1886.

Originally, it was a German theatre.

The famous Czech composer Bedřich Smetana was the director of the opera house until 1882.

The building was designed by the famous architects from Vienna, Hermann Helmer and Ferdinand Fellner.

On the pediment of the Classical façade there is a coach of Dionysos and Thalia portrayed and until the end of the Second World War, there were the busts of Mozart, Goethe and Schiller displayed.

Old statue of St Wenceslas (Vyšehrad)

Opera House

110

The German Theatre Society was inspired with the enthusiasm connected with building of the Czech National Theatre, which was financed by private donations and public collections. The German Theatre was opened on 5th January 1888 with the opera "Master Singers of Nuremberg" by famous German composer Richard Wagner and the German Theatre became very soon a favourite place for the German-speaking actors. Angelo Neumann, a famous opera-director from Bremen (Germany) knew how to establish a German stage of over-regional significance in Prague.

The Main Train Station (Wilson train Station)

[Hlavní nádraží, Wilsonova, Praha 1]

It is an Art Noveau building dating from 1901–1909 and it was built after designs by Josef Fanta. It used to be called Franz Joseph Train Station.

The green area with trees opposite the Main Train Station is the Vrchlický Park. It is the rest of the former municipal park, which was of great elegance and beauty even at the beginning of the 20th century. However, it has completely lost its charm in the 1970s due to certain measures carried out by the municipal authorities.

Cafe in the Main Station

Main Train Station

Na Příkopě Street

[Na Příkopě]

One of the main business, shopping and promenade arteries between the Powder Tower and Můstek. It links up with the lower part of the Wenceslas Square. The street originated on the site of a filled-in water ditch (hence its name: "On the ditch", Na Příkopě). The street also represents the boundary between the Old Town and the new Town.

The Czech National Bank (Na Příkopě 28) was built in 1938 on the site of two hotels with long tradition called At the Blue Star and At the Black Horse. Prominent personalities as Hector Berlioz, Richard Wagner, Fjodor Dostojewski or Carl Spitzweg stayed in the hotels once. At the Blue Star Hotel the Prague Peace Treaty was signed by the Emperor Wilhelm and the Prince Bismarck on 23rd August 1866.

Former German House in Na Příkopě Street (Na Příkopě 22) is called the Slavonic House since 1945. Originally a Baroque Palace was rebuilt in a Classical style in 1798 and it served as a social and cultural life of the German inhabitants of Prague since 1873.

Many German societies and clubs had their meeting and sessions there. Famous writers, for example Detlef von Liliencron,

At the Hibernians [U Hybernů, Náměstí Republiky, Praha 1]

Originally there was a Benedictine Monastery built in 1359. In 1599 the Irish Franciscans (Ireland, Lat. Hibernia, hence the Hibernians) settled here since they have been expelled from their country during the reign of the Queen Elizabeth. Some of the monks went back to Ireland and then brought potatoes to Bohemia in the first half of the 18th century. This building has one of the most outstanding Empire façade in Prague. It originated after the reconstruction of a former Baroque Church (1808). After the secularisation of the church, the building served as the main customs-office. Since 1940s, important national exhibitions and trade markets take place there.

Na Příkopě Street (about 1920)

Rainer Maria Rilke and Gerhart Hauptmann read from their books in the Mirror Hall of the German House. In 1895, the world-known woman-pacifist Bertha von Suttner was invited by the Concordia Society to deliver a speech in this house.

In the former Piarist-Prep School (Na Příkopě 16) studied famous personalities, e.g. Bernard Bolzano, Franz Werfel, Max Brod, Rainer Maria Rilke and Karel Hynek Mácha.

The National Theatre
[Narodní divadlo]

The theatre was solemnly opened on 15th of June 1881 with the opera "Libuše" by Bedřich Smetana. However, the building burned down two months later. After, two years, you could hear there "Libuše" again, in a house built from collected money.

It is the most beautiful example of Czech architecture of the second half of the 19th century and the so-called Generation of the National Theatre took part at decorating of the building.

The New Stage of the National Theatre built in the 1970s from Cuban marble plates and from glass has been even today very controversial from the architectural point of view. The building houses today the famous "Laterna Magica".

Memorial to Božena Němcová

National Theatre in the vicinity of the Vltava river

113

The Church Of SS Cyrill and Methodius

[Kostel sv. Cyrila a Metoděje, Resslova, Praha 2]

One of the Baroque churches dedicated formerly to St Charles Boromaeus was built by Kilian Ignaz Dientzenhofer in about 1740.

The Czech parachutists, who killed Reinhard Heydrich, the Deputy Reich Protector of Bohemia, in May 1942 used the crypt of the church as a hiding place. On the 18th of June 1942 none of the resistance fighters survived.

There is a tablet bearing their names to commemorate those brave parachutists.

Mánes (Masarykovo nábřeží – Masaryk Embankment)

114

Ginger [Rogers] and Fred [Astaire] Building

[Tančící dům, Rašínovo nábřeží 80, Praha 2]

The much-debated office building, an example of modern futuristic architecture, was completed in 1994, under the auspices of the president Václav Havel who owned the property. The design of Vlado Milunic was co-authored by am American architect Frank O. Gehry and the building was erected on a lot that had been levelled with the ground during an American air raid in February 1945.

The building might seem a bit disturbing since you may find out that it does not correspond with the central European building tradition.

The clock of the famous "U Fleků" pub
(detail of the façade)

Ginger [Rogers] and Fred [Astaire] Building

The New Town Hall
[Karlovo náměstí, Praha 2]

The Town Hall of the New Town founded by Charles IV is situated on the square originally called the Cattle Market. The New Town Hall was built in a Gothic style. On 30th July 1419, the first Prague defenestration took place there.

It gained a prominent place in Czech history in 1419 when the Hussites hurled the Catholic councillors from the windows of the New Town Hall. It was this defenestration that initiated the Hussite revolutionary uprising, which made the ruling King Wenceslas IV very angry.

The Outer Districts of Prague

Vyšehrad

[Vyšehrad]

The Vyšehrad citadel, situated on a rock overlooking the Vltava River, is a Baroque fortress that lies in the south of Prague. It is believed that an old-Slavic castle used to be in that area already in 800 AD. First written references are in a chronicle from the year 1002. In the course of its 1000 years long history, Vyšehrad was a king's residence, spiritual centre of the country (the Vyšehrad provost was beside the archbishop the second most important person within the church hierarchy), a Baroque fortress and a trip destination for the inhabitants of the big city. Many buildings and monuments remind us of the rich history of the hill.

At the Vyšehrad Cemetery

Libuše's Bath is supposed to be the place where the prophetess Libuše walked through when going to take bath in the Vltava river.

The Leopold Gate reminds us of the fact that Vyšehrad was a powerful military fortress once.

The Old Deanery (Soběslavova Street 1) used to be the residence of the deans. In 1760, it was badly damaged during a powder explosion.

The New Deanery (Štulcova Street 4) was built between 1872-1874 thanks to the important provost Václav Štulc in a Neo-Gothic style.

The Slavín is the most respectable part of the Vyšehrad Cemetery. Many reputable personalities of the Czech history are buried there: Czech writer and poet Jan Neruda, Czech painter Alfons Mucha, Czech composer Bedřich Smetana etc.

St Martin rotunda dates from the 11th century and hence it is the oldest preserved rotunda in Prague.

The emblem of the Vyšehrad Chapter

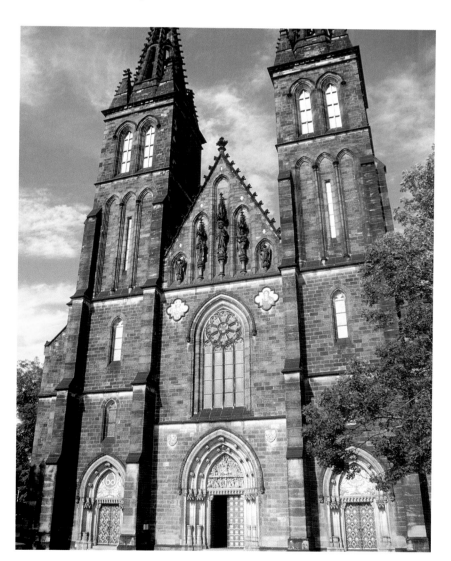

Ruins of the Libušin Baths

The Church of SS Peter and Paul has a building history that goes back to the Middle Ages. At the beginning of the 20th century was the façade renewed and a new neo-Gothic portal was made. One of the notable features of the interior is a panel – painting copy of the "Madonna of the Rain".

Bertramka – Mozart Museum

[Bertramka, Mozartova 169, Praha 5]

In this suburban villa Mozart stayed with his friends, the Dušeks, during his frequent visits to Prague.

His opera "Don Giovanni" is supposed to have been finished here and was then given its world premiere in the Theatre of the Estates on October 29th, 1787.

The villa today serves as the most important Mozart museum, the exposition is to be found in seven rooms where you can follow Mozart's stay in Prague thoroughly.

You will also find there the piano that Mozart was supposed to play himself.

Mozart's statue in the Na Bertramce Park

Where Mozart used to stay as a guest: Bertramka Villa in the Prague suburb of Smíchov

St Margaret Benedictine Monastery

[Klášter sv. Markéty v Břevnově, Bělohorská 1, Praha 6]

St Adalbert, the second bishop of Prague founded the monastery in 992, and it is the oldest monastery in Prague.

The Prelate's Hall has a ceiling fresco by Cosmas Damian Asam, the Master of south German Late Baroque, "St Gunther death".

Christoph Dientzenhofer built the church at the beginning of the 18th century.

The early Romanesque crypt of the church is still preserved. The altarpieces were made by Peter Brandl (The deaths of St Gunther and of St Benedict).

Summer Hill
[Letná]

The name already reveals the fact that especially in summer, the Summer Hill was a favourite destination of the inhabitants of Prague. When strolling up there, you will go by many interesting places, such as the Kramář Villa (the residence of the Prime Minister); the Hanau Pavilion made on the occasion of the jubilee Industrial Exhibition in Prague in 1891. The plateau also supported the biggest Stalin monument in the world once, but the statue was pulled down in 1962.

At the Letná area, every year on the 1st of May during the communist regime, the state power was to be shown here in mass parades and marches. In November 1989, thousands of people demonstrated against the communist regime.

The gates to the Břevnov Monastery

The Kramář Villa

119

The Hvězda Preserve with Summer Palace

[Letohrádek Hvězda, Obora Hvězda, Praha 6]

Emperor Ferdinand I established here a hunting preserve in 1530.

His son, the Archduke Ferdinand of Tyrol, had built here the royal Hvězda Summer Palace in 1555 in a Renaissance style and its ground plan is of a six-pointed star.

You will find there rich stucco decorations by Paolo della Stella.

The Hvězda Preserve lies below the White Mountain where the legendary battle took place.

Today in the Hvězda Summer Palace is the Alois Jirásek (1851–1930) and Mikoláš Aleš (1852–1913) Museum.